Honest
Abe Lincoln

Easy-to-Read Stories
about Abraham Lincoln

by DAVID A. ADLER

illustrated by JOHN WALLNER

Holiday House / New York

"Most folks are about as happy as they make their minds to be."—*Abraham Lincoln*

Reading Level: 2.7

Text copyright © 2009 by David A. Adler
Illustrations copyright © 2009 by John Wallner
All Rights Reserved
HOLIDAY HOUSE is registered in the U.S. Patent and
Trademark Office.
Printed and Bound in Malaysia
www.holidayhouse.com
First Edition
1 3 5 7 9 10 8 6 4 2

Library of Congress Cataloging-in-Publication Data
Adler, David A.
Honest Abe Lincoln : easy-to-read stories about
Abraham Lincoln / by David A. Adler ;
illustrated by John Wallner. — 1st ed.
p. cm.
Includes bibliographical references.
ISBN-13: 978-0-8234-2057-5 (hardcover)
1. Lincoln, Abraham, 1809-1865—Anecdotes—Juvenile
literature. 2. Presidents—United States—Biography—
Anecdotes—Juvenile literature. I. Wallner, John C., ill.
II. Title.
E457.905.A345 2008
973.7092—dc22
[B]
2007044285

Contents

1. Abraham Lincoln

Abraham Lincoln was born in Kentucky in 1809.

He was born in a small log cabin.

The cabin had a dirt floor.

It had just one window.
Young Abraham Lincoln
chopped wood.
He plowed and planted.

When he plowed,

he often took along a book.

He would stop so his horse could rest

and he could read.

Later, Abraham Lincoln

worked in a store.

He was also a lawyer and congressman.

In 1860 he was elected president.

2. Honest Abe Lincoln

In 1831 Abraham Lincoln worked
in Denton Offut's store.
One evening a woman
bought half a pound of tea.
Early the next morning
Lincoln checked the scales.

He found a problem.

He knew he had not given the woman
a full half pound.

Before he even ate his breakfast,
he walked a long way to her house.

He gave her the missing tea.

Another time,
at the end of the day,
he checked his bills.
He found one woman
had paid too much.
Abraham Lincoln closed the store.
He walked almost three miles
to return what she had overpaid—
six and a quarter cents.

From then on
many people called him
Honest Abe Lincoln.

3. Post Office in a Hat

In 1833 Abraham Lincoln was made
postmaster of New Salem, Illinois.
Letters and newspapers
were brought to him.
He would keep the mail
until people came for it.

As postmaster, Lincoln could read
newspapers for free.
He liked that.
The people of New Salem
liked having him as their postmaster.
If an important letter came,
he rushed to deliver it.

Sometimes he went a few miles
to bring someone a letter.
Lincoln did not like
sitting all day in his office.
He often went out.

But before he did,

he put the mail

inside his hat.

He looked for people he knew.

If he had a letter or newspaper for them,

he took off his hat

and delivered the mail.

4. Stuck in Mud

As a young lawyer,
Abraham Lincoln rode on horseback.
He rode from one town to the next.
One day
he rode past a muddy field.
He saw a pig there, stuck in the mud.
Lincoln was wearing a new suit.
He did not want to ruin it,
so he rode on.

As he rode, he thought about the pig.

After two miles he stopped.

He rode back and saved the pig.

Lincoln got back on his horse.

Now his clothes were muddy.

He told himself
he did it all for the pig.
Later, he said, he knew
he really did it for himself.
He said he could never have been happy
if he had not saved the pig.

5. A Talent for Hunting

Abraham Lincoln liked to say
that some people just have a talent.
He often told of a man named Jake.
Jake had a talent for hunting.
His gun was old and rusted.
But each day that he went hunting
he came back with an armload of birds.
"Jake, how do you do it?"
someone asked.

"Oh, I just do it," Jake said.

"But *how* do you do it?"

Jake did not want to tell.

"It is a secret," he said.

"I will keep your secret,"
the other man said.

Jake leaned close.

"You won't tell?" he asked.

"No, I won't."

"Well," Jake said.
"What I do is hide by a fence
and make a noise like a turnip.
That brings the birds."
Jake laughed.

Surely when Lincoln told this story,
he laughed too.
Of course, Abraham Lincoln was right.
Some people just have a talent.
Abraham Lincoln had a talent
for telling stories.

6. Why Abraham Lincoln Grew a Beard

It was October 1860.

Soon there would be an election.

Grace Bedell wrote to Lincoln.

"I am a little girl only 11 years old,

but want you should be President."

She wrote that he would look better

with a beard.

Grace Bedell had four older brothers.
"Part of them will vote for you,"
she wrote.
"If you let your whiskers grow
I will try and get the rest of them
to vote for you."

In November 1860 Abraham Lincoln
was elected president.
In February 1861
he was on his way to Washington.

His train stopped in Westfield, New York.

Grace lived there.

A large crowd came to the train station.

They wanted to see the new president.

He had a beard now.

He asked to meet Grace.

"There she is,"

a boy in the crowd called out.

Lincoln stepped down from the train.

He took Grace Bedell's hand.

He kissed her cheek.

"You see," he said.

"I let my whiskers grow for you."

7. President Abraham Lincoln

Abraham Lincoln hated slavery.
In 1860, in the South,
there were more than three million
African American slaves.
People there were not happy
to have a president who hated slavery.
Soon after Lincoln was elected,
eleven Southern states
broke away from the United States.

They would form their own country.
Abraham Lincoln led the war
to keep the country together.
It has been called the
War between the States
and the Civil War.
The war lasted four years.
Many died.

The war ended on April 9, 1865.

The nation was one again.

The slaves were free.

Five days later

Abraham Lincoln was at the theater.

An actor who was not happy that
the South had lost the war
shot the president.
Abraham Lincoln died the next day.

A train took his body home to Illinois.
Many Americans
stood outside to watch
as the train passed.
They stood and said good-bye
to Honest Abe Lincoln.

Important Dates

February 12, 1809
Abraham Lincoln is born in Kentucky.

1831
Lincoln works as a clerk in Denton Offut's store.

1833
Lincoln appointed postmaster of New Salem, Illinois.

November 4, 1842
Lincoln marries Mary Todd.
Later they have four sons: Robert, Edward,
William, and Thomas (Tad).

November 6, 1860
Lincoln is elected president.

April 12, 1861
The first shots of the Civil War are fired
at Fort Sumter, South Carolina.

April 14, 1865
President Abraham Lincoln is shot. He dies the next day.

Sources

Kunhardt, Philip B., Jr., Philip B. Kunhardt III, and Peter W. Kunhardt. *Lincoln: An Illustrated Biography.* New York: Knopf, 1992.

McClure, Alexander K. *"Abe" Lincoln's Yarns and Stories.* Chicago: The Educational Company, 1901.

McClure, J. B., ed. *Abraham Lincoln's Stories and Speeches.* Chicago: Rhodes and McClure Publishing Company, 1898.

Sandburg, Carl. *Abraham Lincoln: The Prairie and the War Years One Volume Edition.* New York: Harcourt, Brace, 1954.

Notes

Colonel Alexander K. McClure, the author of *"Abe" Lincoln's Yarns and Stories*, was a newspaperman and a Pennsylvania politician. On the title page of his book about Lincoln, he is said to have been "a personal friend and advisor of the story telling president."

Chapter Four: The streets were not paved in many of the towns Lincoln visited. After a heavy rain dirt roads often became thick with mud.

Chapter Five: The quotes are from Alexander K. McClure's book, page 116.

Chapter Six: The quotes from Grace Bedell's letter are from the Kundhardts' book, page 13.